Learning the Hard Way

Part-time Degree Students and the University of Toronto

By Deanne Fisher

Published by: The Association of Part-time
Undergraduate Students of the University of Toronto

Toronto, 1995

Tel (416) 978-3993 / Fax (416) 971-1393

Canadian Cataloguing in Publication Data

Fisher, Deanne, 1965-
Learning the Hard Way: Part-time Degree Students and the University of Toronto

Includes bibiliographical references and index.
ISBN 0-9699678-0-2

1. University of Toronto - Students.
2. Students, - Part-time - Ontario - Toronto.
3. Adult education - Ontario - Toronto.
I. University of Toronto. Association of Part-time Undergraduate Students.
II. Title.
LC5305.T67F5 1995   378'.198'09713541 C95-931602-7

Cataloguing in Publication Data

Preface

E very day seems idyllic during the Summer Session at the University of Toronto. Being surrounded by others who have given up their warm summer days and evenings to sit in a climate-controlled classroom or library gives a student a sense of comraderie one doesn't often feel during the rest of the year. On one such splendid day, I approached Woodsworth College, the home base for most of U of T's adult part-time (and some full-time) students. I was worried when I saw a Metropolitan Police car parked in the bike lane on St. George Street outside the College. The University's own police force is not able to deal with serious incidents, so the presence of Metro police usually means trouble.

Fortunately, I was wrong. Just inside the doors of the College stood a police officer, enrolment papers in hand, waiting in line at the registrar's office along with a dozen other students.

When I arrived the next day, I found a Toronto Hydro truck parked outside. I had learned from my experience of the day before: I did not suspect a power failure. Sure enough, the driver of the vehicle, in hard hat and coveralls, stood in the registration line-up.

After four years of working and studying at the University of Toronto and Woodsworth College, my fascination with the diversity of the part-time student population has not diminished. I have become only more amazed that so many people have enough motivation to attend university for so many years despite the challenges they face.

These students have chosen to study at the University of Toronto knowing that it won't be easy, or cheap, or quick. They accept this when they register for the first course on a long road to a certificate, diploma or degree. They rearrange their lives to prepare for what will be expected of them. But they have expectations of their own, as well. And they are not a complacent lot. When the University or the government appears to be erecting further roadblocks in front of them, they holler.

This book is a tempered holler about the state of the University of Toronto's commitment to adult education. It is a book written very much in the tradition of the Association of Part-time Undergraduate Students—restrained but passionate.

To prevent the book from being too restrained, I have included the voices of the part-time students themselves. Throughout this book are samples of the thousands of comments APUS received from students when the organization conducted its Student Survey in 1991. The survey, mailed to almost 18,000 fall and summer students, received an impressive response rate of 17 per cent. These comments were virtually unsolicited — a few blank lines had been put on the end of the survey to fill some empty space. The response to the survey demonstrated that part-time students had a lot to say. APUS, and I, have long sought a way to present their comments in the context of the issues they raised, and to pass them on to a wider audience. With this book, we hope we have found that forum.

Table of Contents

Introduction

THE LIFELONG LEARNING SOCIETY

T|his book assumes that Canadian universities have a central role to play in the national enterprise of creating a society of lifelong learners. This role has been recognized, though hardly defined, by policy-makers and shapers at both the federal and provincial levels of government. While it is understood that formal learning must be available to and embraced by adults throughout their working lives, there remain important distinctions between the sort of learning thought to be appropriate for younger students, and the sort more suited to the "adult", working population.[1]

Traditionally, universities have served adults by extending limited expertise and facilities to them in the form of non-credit, "continuing education" courses. Adults have been expected to study computers, though not computer

---

[1] The term 'adult' will be used throughout this book to refer to students older than the traditional university student age of 18-24 or those students, of any age, with the additional responsibilities one associates with adulthood. The use of this term is not meant to imply that younger students are not adults. Alternatives to this terminology, however, were thought to be even more objectionable. The use of the term 'mature' student implies others are immature. The use of the term 'non-traditional' implies all younger students are traditional, which is clearly not true given the diversity of the population. The term 'older' student was considered ambiguous and inappropriate to describe students in their late 20's and 30's.

science; languages, but not linguistics. In other words, the educational needs of adults have long been thought to be practical, not theoretical, in nature.

Such distinctions have served adult students well in the past and continue to provide substantial benefits. Somewhat autonomous continuing education units, housed within universities, offer courses designed with the working adult in mind. But in a society which treats knowledge as capital, the distinction between "training" and "learning" is becoming increasingly blurred. Adults can no longer be relegated to purely practical subjects, nor can youth be relegated to theoretical study, partly because theory and practice themselves cannot be so neatly defined. The role of universities in a society of lifelong learners must be to provide learning opportunities, based on aptitude and initiative, to students of any age, physical ability, family status, and financial means.

Whether the University of Toronto has acknowledged and embraced this role is a question this book considers from the perspective of the students themselves. Whether Canadian universities in general will fulfil this role without government intervention is beyond the scope of this book; it remains, however, a pertinent question for readers as they consider the experience and lessons of the last 20 years at the U of T.

Despite all of the evidence that Canada's competitiveness is intimately linked to the knowledge of its citizens, and that one university degree no longer provides a lifelong basis for a career, doubts about the merits of lifelong learning persist. Decades of debate have provided us with clear and compelling arguments to show why universities must provide degree programs for academically capable Canadians in all stages of life.

The social betterment argument. The conviction that to be a student, of any age, is to participate in the improvement of society as a whole is precisely what motivated some of Canada's oldest universities, including U of T, to provide opportunities for adult learners.

Somewhat obscured of late by our economic obsessions, the notion that learning is both ageless and invaluable was perhaps best articulated in 1954 by one of the United Kingdom's most articulate supporters of adult education — Sir Winston Churchill:

> "I have no doubt myself that a man or woman earnestly seeking in grown-up life to be guided to wide and suggestive knowledge in its largest and most uplifted sphere will make the best of all the pupils in this age of clatter and buzz, of gape and gloat. The appetite of adults to be shown the foundations and processes of thought will never be denied by a British administration cherishing the continuity of our Island life."*(Blyth,* p. 194)

The demography argument. The age group upon which the university system traditionally relies for the bulk of its enrolment — 18 to 24 year-olds — is shrinking in Canada. The baby boom has passed this prime undergraduate age and although a greater proportion of young people are seeking access to universities, their declining numbers are predicted to more than offset this increase in the participation rate. In other words, universities will have no choice but to cater to an older market if they wish to maintain current enrolments. Some might argue that reduced enrolments will be a welcome relief from the pressures caused by decades of expansion. However, since universities are, to some extent, financially dependent on the number of students, a drastic change in enrolment policy is unlikely.

The social justice argument. Whether or not a young person aspires to a university degree is largely dependent upon the potential student's family background, and in particular, whether her or his parents attended university. Numerous studies have demonstrated this cycle; some researchers suggest that parental education and income are the two most influential factors in a young person's consideration of higher education. (*Levin,* 52) A much smaller proportion of adult students comes from highly educated families (*Anisef,* 14); for many of these students, entry into university at a later age represents a "second chance", after they have been discouraged or inadvertently dissuaded in their youth from pursuing either university admission or the high school prerequisites. Granted, these students still represent a minority of part-time learners at the University of Toronto (about 30 per cent) and other institutions, but their numbers stand to grow as programs and services emerge to enable adults to test their abilities in an academic environment. Academic bridging programs for those lacking the high school prerequisites have proven to be an effective means of both providing access and ensuring success for students otherwise unlikely to attend university.

More than one report on the restructuring of social programs has suggested that government support for individuals might be contingent on the recipient's efforts to complete training or education programs, including those at the university level. For many years, the higher education community has sought a means to diversify its student base — to end the cycle of privilege in which an individual's chances of attending university are largely determined by cultural or socio-economic background. Though it certainly does not eliminate the barriers to university for underprivileged young people, the option of a second chance through admission as an adult student has brought a measure of social equity to the system.

The economic arguments. By providing individuals with the chance to develop their own potential, we create a more capable and adaptable workforce, and thereby strengthen the economy as a whole. The advantages to government and to the Canadian economy of providing access for adults to university degree programs have never been more obvious.

A number of trends which demonstrate the economic benefits of a highly educated workforce have been documented by Statistics Canada and economists. First, unemployment rates among the university-educated are significantly lower than for those lacking a degree. Even during the worst of the recession of the early 1990s, employment among those with a university degree grew while it stabilized or fell for those with less education. (*HRD Canada,* January 1994) Second, even when they do become unemployed, the university-educated are generally the first to become re-employed. And finally, income gaps between the educated and those without higher education are widening. Economists, such as U of T's David Nowlan, predict these trends will continue as Canada moves deeper into a knowledge-based and service-oriented economy:

> "One of the reasons for the relative success of university graduates is that they are active principally in the growing rather than the declining job categories and economic sectors." (*Nowlan*, 14)

The Canadian economy is in flux, as is its adult workforce. The bulk of the literature points to higher education as the key to a more adaptable workforce. The problem of high unemployment for those who lack a post-secondary education is not unique to young people and cannot be solved with university programs exclusive to the young. The rhetoric of lifelong learning heard from all political parties in the federal election of 1993 will become a reality only if universities adapt to meet the needs of adult students.

The supply and demand argument. The number of part-time learners in university degree programs in Canada steadily increased for decades before it recently dropped. There are now over a quarter of a million part-time undergraduate students in Canada. Clearly, the Canadian public understands the value of a university degree and sees no reason why it should not be accessible to those who happen to have the concurrent responsibilities of a job or family. Moreover, the business community places increasing demands on universities to better serve its need for an educated labour force, producing tools and hosting conferences to assist educational institutions in providing marketable graduates. There are some indications that, if the university system is unwilling to be the supplier, business will simply assume the role of the provider of adult education. The Bank of Montreal, for example, recently established its own "university" to train and re-train its employees. Private vocational schools are aggressively recruiting students on the basis that their programs are more suited to the needs of a changing workplace and adult lifestyles.

Many in the university community would be content to see the private sector take over responsibility for what is clearly training and leave universities to concentrate on the expansion of knowledge, unsullied by the demands of commerce. A more pragmatic approach would admit that there is an element of training in all education and that it is possible for universities to maintain their academic integrity while making an effort to serve the needs of the labour market.

The return-on-investment argument. Though this motive may seem cynical, access for adult learners to the university's core programs is often argued to be useful in building public support. The ultimate goal is to enlist taxpayer support for higher education and, even more important these days, to create a new source of higher income donors for university fundraising campaigns.

All of these arguments should give universities the impetus to provide a more varied array of learning opportunities to adults. But none of this should be taken to mean that the education of adults is of greater importance than the education of our youth. Indeed, both generations stand to benefit from changes to the traditional methods of delivering education. The distinction between the "traditional" and "adult" student populations has become less and less significant as the needs of the two groups converge. Moreover, it has become an annoying and artificial obstacle to making changes in the delivery of university education that would enhance access and quality for both groups. Never have the needs of two so-called "distinct" groups been so compatible.

Similarly, the emphasis here on credit courses and degree programs is not meant to denigrate the important role of universities in providing non-credit courses to the community, but to acknowledge that non-credit activities are not the intellectual, social or economic equivalent of a degree.

Aside from extolling the virtues of lifelong learning, I make one other assumption in this book which might be controversial: that part-time programs are the most logical route for adult learners to gain access to university degree programs. It may be that there are other ways to achieve the same end. Perhaps, for example, if most adults were offered financial support to study full-time, they would eagerly accept. Indeed, many adults already make the sacrifices necessary to study full-time. But part-time study remains the most popular method of pursuing university education for Canada's adults, and it remains the only program in which we have enough experience to assess our successes and failures. The university's acceptance of adult learners in this capacity represents a test case for the feasibility of any other methods.

There are few people in academic or policy circles who question the benefits of lifelong learning. The challenge in stimulating change within the system is to find ways to transfer widespread support for lifelong learning into tangible improvements in the educational experience of adult students. That process inevitably involves demands on resources and shifts in priorities which many are not yet prepared to make. The struggle to turn the concept of lifelong learning into a reality and to create opportunities for non-traditional students has guided the Association of Part-time Undergraduate Students at the U of T for the past twenty-five years. It is relatively easy to convince political leaders, the public and even university administrators of the importance of creating learning opportunities for the adult population. It is a much more difficult task to convince them that they have not yet succeeded.

Chapter One.

TAKING CREDIT

T he University of Toronto is an institution which approaches change with caution. When presented with an opportunity to change, it rarely leaps at the chance. Rather, it studies, considers, deliberates, examines, reports and, eventually, implements. While U of T's institutional inertia has frustrated many advocates of change, this conservative approach has also protected it from passing fancies and political bandwagons which could have threatened its integrity in the long run. It is not surprising then, that at the beginning of a boom in adult education in the late 1960s and early 1970s, the University of Toronto would react with some hostility to the demands of a newly organized group of part-time degree students. What is remarkable is the uncharacteristic speed with which the University responded to, and eventually met, these students' demands. Their swift political success was the result of skilful lobbying, good luck, and most of all, the sheer logic of their arguments.

To some degree, adult and part-time learners had been part
of the U of T tradition long before they became politically
organized. They had been there since 1894, recognized
through a Statute of the University Senate which dictated
that "No part of the expense incurred for... University
Extension shall be a charged on the ordinary revenue of the
University." The ambiguity of the Statute's definition of
"extension" ensured that for 75 years, part-time students,
whether they were merely interested in some professional
upgrading or engaged in an intense
course of study that paralleled a full-
time, "regular" degree program, were
relegated to the Division of University
Extension, which operated on a
cost-recovery basis through student fees and was widely
considered to be an adjunct to the primary mission of the
University.

> "I am a mature student achieving a life time desire to attend university. My motive is to keep my brain working and to learn more about the world I live in...."

By the late 1960s, the differences between two distinct types
of students registered in the Division of Extension had
become clear. Part-time degree students, growing rapidly in
number, were now well enough organized to express objec-
tions to their status. They pointed out the similarities
between their own academic responsibilities and those of
the full-time student body, and to their incompatibility with
the Division of Extension's other members — the non-credit students. Although part-time degree students resembled
the non-credit, continuing education students in age, work
and family situation, it was the nature of their scholarly
endeavours — the subject matter, the intensity and duration
of their academic commitment — which should, they

argued, warrant treatment more like that enjoyed by the younger, full-time undergraduate students.

This plea for equitable treatment — in particular, for access to publicly-funded courses and services for part-time degree students — was supported by a number of administrators and academics and swiftly caught the attention of the entire university community. By 1970, the year of a groundbreaking Report on the Division of Extension, the number of students seeking a degree through part-time study had grown to well over 8,000, a jump of more than 15 per cent from the previous year. The Report of the Presidential Advisory Committee on Extension — the PACE Report — at long last exposed the hypocrisy of the situation:

> "....It is a two-way experience meeting young people with the same goals and in return I sometimes add a different viewpoint to discussions."
> **Woodsworth College, female, age: 60**

"The ambiguities and ambivalence described can be seen most corrosively at work in the use of 'Extension student' in its present derogatory, descriptive, apologetic, resentful, messianic, and demarcatory senses. It is time to question the distinction between students thought to be fully in the University and those taken to be only half-in. It is also necessary to make choices between those of the University's activities proper to it and those merely tolerated through inertia, or misguided notions of public relations. The first step, then is to discard the word 'Extension' and to stop talking about the 'Extension student'." (*PACE*, 10)

The Report went on to recommend the closure of the
Division of Extension and the full integration of part-time
degree students into all of the Faculties and Schools of the
University, as well as the existing college structure of the
Faculty of Arts and Science.

Despite emerging provincial policies which made clear the
government's commitment to part-time university
education and which, conveniently enough, provided
financial incentives to integrate part- and
full-time students, the University of
Toronto moved forward with its typical
caution. Historian J.A. Blyth, in his
account of the end of the Division of
University Extension, *A Foundling at
Varsity*, described the University's response to the PACE
Report this way:

> "It is unfortunate that part-
> time university studies are
> often downgraded (in
> comparison to full-time
> studies) in some people's
> perceptions."
> **New College, male, age: 22**

> "...(S)ome individuals seemed to imagine that ten
> thousand barbarians were about to invade the
> temples of learning. It was quite possible, for
> example, that part-time students could outnumber
> regular day students and produce a need to change
> cherished routines. There was particular concern
> that established time tables would be upset."(*Blyth*,
> 170)

The PACE Report, and its supporters, had dared to
challenge one of the University's most treasured notions of
undergraduate study: they suggested that full-time study
may not, in fact, be the ideal. The idea that full-time

devotion to academic work represented the most appropriate method of study was deeply embedded in the university's practices. To suggest that students could afford to be distracted by other activities challenged a widely valued concept of student life.

Proponents of integration believed that all students could and should expect to carry out other activities while pursuing a degree. They argued that integration would not only benefit part-time students but would give full-time students the flexibility to study when they wanted to and at a pace that allowed for other activities or responsibilities. For part-time students, these arguments were secondary. For them, the ultimate benefit of integration would be the end of

> "I find it at times frustrating to be a part-time student. It seems that part-time students are not part of U of T."
> Woodsworth College, female, age: 28

what had effectively become a second tier degree; a degree earned on a part-time basis would no longer be distinguishable from one earned full-time.

Around the same time that PACE began its work, the Association of Part-time Undergraduate Degree Students (APUDS) was born. Perhaps because the University community greeted its creation with such a flurry of debate on the very issues it sought to address and because the University had so long been in need of a voice for its rapidly expanding mass of adult learners, APUDS quickly became a significant political force. This was true both within the University and, most importantly, at Queen's Park where the plight of the part-time student received great sympathy. Blyth described APUDS as a group "accustomed to being first-class citizens and taxpayers during the day" and irritated by the "third-class" treatment afforded to them as evening and summer students at U of T. (*Blyth*, 146) They used their collective power as taxpayers, as well as some fairly sophisticated lobbying techniques, to achieve, in a matter of a few years, the integration of their members into the general undergraduate curriculum and the integration of their political voice into the general decision-making processes and bodies of the University. Part-time students were given designated seats on University committees, boards, and even its highest decision-making body, the Governing Council. And APUDS, which became the Association of Part-time Undergraduate Students (APUS) in 1971, began to demand the same recognition and respect afforded to its almost 60-year-old full-time counterpart — the Students' Administrative Council.

> "It is very difficult to complete an undergraduate degree at U of T on a part-time basis. The only reason I am not taking a course this semester is that I couldn't find one on either the Erindale or St. George Campus."
> Erindale College, female, age: 33

In the early 1970s, the University community awaited, with a mixture of anticipation and anxiety, a virtual revolution in programs, services, pedagogical methods, and culture.

The provincial Minister of University Affairs predicted, in his annual report for 1970-1971 "a trend towards part-time studies, a shift in the emphasis that can be expected to pervade the entire post-secondary system." (*Blyth, 170*) The University's less traditional divisions welcomed the change. Scarborough College, whose Dean, S.J. Colman, had served as Chair of PACE, led the road to integration, providing a consolidated course timetable and evening access to all of its services and facilities. Erindale College, in its response to the PACE Report, resolved that "full-time study be regarded as a 'norm' rather than an ideal."(*Erindale Response to PACE*) Innis College, the newest college on the St. George Campus, began to admit part-time students in the fall of 1972.

The growing support for the University's role in adult education caused the Director of the Division of Extension at the time, E.M. Gruetzner, to make some bold predictions in his annual report for 1971-1972:

> **"Course availability and competition for courses and textbooks has made my U of T experience one of the worst in my academic career.**
> **Too many people for too few resources."**
> **Woodsworth College, female, age: 27**

"When the student attends will not be important; the distinction between full- and part-time will disappear; the lock-step resident prerequisites programmes will assume less importance. With the four-day work-week, the week-end university for residence and tutorials will be established." (*Gruetzner*, 81)

Although the Faculty of Arts and Science on the St. George Campus, the largest single division in the University, had yet to come to terms with the recommendations of the PACE Report — and indeed would require another two committees and reports before it would — the Director of the Division of Extension felt confident that his arguments would win the support of his colleagues. "Learning knows no barrier of age, of hours from nine to five, of an eight-month 'academic year'," he wrote. "Rather ... it is a continuing lifelong process." (*Gruetzner,* 82) In 1974, the Division of Extension, APUS and many others believed that part-time students had been fully accepted by the University of Toronto when it opened Woodsworth College—an Arts and Science college designed to serve the unique needs of the University's part-time undergraduate students.

The means by which the University of Toronto chose to meet the demands of its adult learners — integration of full- and part-time degree students — was one of a number of options considered. Other universities grappling with these issues around the same time chose other routes. York University, opened only a decade before the issue fully emerged at U of T, had largely rejected the centralized, integrated model in favour of a separate unit — Atkinson College — which not only looked after the non-academic needs of its part-time students, but was responsible for co-ordinating specialized part-time academic programs as well. This model had significant advantages: its teaching styles were tailored to the adult learner, students were guaranteed that the programs could be completed through evening and summer study, and it offered the comfort of studying with older classmates. But such a model would have been self-defeating at U of T, where part-time students needed to demonstrate they could live-up to the institution's long-established rigorous standards. APUS was astute enough to recognize that nothing short of complete

> "I think the biggest problems facing the university involve the degradation of services offered. Course selections have been whittled away to the minimum leaving little of variety or interest."
> University College,
> male, age: 23

integration, in which courses were open to both full- and part-time students, taught by the same instructors and leading to the same degree in the same program, would prove they were up to the challenge. Only integration would bring the part-time student above second class status in the community. APUS was relentless in pursuing this goal and had secured the structural and policy context necessary to achieve it within a few short years of the organization's creation.

After five years of tumultuous change, and now that the stage had been set for the natural blending of routine and innovation, it might have been expected

> "I am extremely grateful for the opportunity of further-ing my knowledge as a senior, part-time student."
> Woodsworth College, male, age: 66

that APUS would take a breather from its obsession with the integration of part-time students. Faculty would adjust to the diversity of age and experience in their class-rooms over time. University administrators would contin-ue to implement the changes required to achieve an equality of treatment for both full- and part-time students. Services would evolve and expand to meet the needs of the University's dramatically changed student popula-tion. APUS, encouraged by its recent successes, moved promptly to pursue the interests of part-time students beyond the boundaries of the Faculty of Arts and Science and, indeed, beyond the University of Toronto. It spearheaded the creation of a national lobby group — the Canadian Organization of Part-time University Students (COPUS) — to tackle the issue of government financial assistance for part-time students and promote part-time study nationally. In the early 1980s, APUS launched a campaign to create more opportunities for graduate education on a part-time basis, and followed that with a successful effort to create a part-time program in the Faculty of Law. APUS had fought for and attained the responsibilities that come with being one of the central student societies at U of T. With this accomplished, the focus of the organization shifted from its original mandate of ensuring the complete integration of part-time students into the University of Toronto community to a more central role in the process of consultation, debate and policy-making on everything from grading schemes to sexual harassment. APUS welcomed these new responsibilities, determined to ensure that the perspectives of part-time tudents were incorporated into virtually every significant decision.

> "I think APUS helps me feel a bit more connected to UofT. I am a firm believer in accessible, high quality, flexible education and teaching for lifelong learners."
> Victoria College,
> female, age: 35

In the meantime, however, the boom for Ontario universities had ended. By the mid-1980s, the combination of growing enrolment and shrinking funding had made the University's financial position the central issue on campus. And part-time students simply took their place in line with every other constituency concerned about the effects of budget restraint. As courses were cut and hours of service limited, virtually every tangible step forward for part-time students was overshadowed by the slow and largely unintentional erosion of much of what part-time students had gained a decade earlier.

By 1994, the 20th anniversary of Woodsworth College and the 25th anniversary of APUS, the still impressive roster of evening and summer Arts and Science courses had nevertheless failed to grow with the increased demand. Although Woodsworth enjoys an exquisite new building — with an office for APUS nestled comfortably in its rafters — it remains vulnerable to budget cuts, serving the largest number of students of any college, but lacking the residences, faculty members or the history that give other colleges their sense of permanence. The enthusiastic response of the two suburban campuses to the integration of part-time students has deteriorated into a constant struggle to sustain evening and summer programs and to make services accessible. The "weekend" university has yet to materialize and all off-campus, workplace credit courses have now long since been cancelled for financial reasons. Shrinking faculty ranks and leaner administrative and support services, combined with increasing enrolment, have created a climate of anonymity for most students. For part-time students — generally those with the least time to wait in line-ups and least able to adapt to limited lab or office hours — the effects are disastrous.

There have been small successes along the way. Old buildings have been upgraded to include wheelchair ramps and elevators. An emerging focus on meeting the needs of students with children has led to the creation of new child care centres. And a small contingent of Saturday courses reappeared, in the early 1990s, and remains on the Arts and Science timetable. These initiatives have no doubt made the difference between dropping out or forging ahead for a small group of students. And each initiative is testimony to the effect of political will in the context of limited resources. But they do not counteract the gradual deterioration of programs and services which make part-time degree study possible for the vast majority of adult students.

The University of Toronto took a considered and deliberate step forward 25 years ago when it decided that the cause of adult education warranted a dramatic change in University practices. Now it is slipping backward, not because of a considered change of priorities, but because external forces have jeopardized its stated commitment to adult education. At the opening of a child care centre at the University in 1992, U of T President Robert Prichard made a short speech about the need to make institutional commitments and to continue to move forward, even in times of fiscal restraint. His message deserved a much wider audience.

Chapter Two:

A PORTRAIT OF CHANGE:
The Demographics of Part-time Students

I n 1971, in the context of provincial discussions on the issue of integrating part- and full-time students at Ontario universities, the Association of Part-time Undergraduate Students at the University of Toronto issued a statement, which, in retrospect, reads more like a premonition:

> "Integration must not become a stick with which to beat its creators. Nor can we allow it to be deflected from our original objectives so that it serves merely to offer greater choice to the full-time student at the expense of the part-time student."

For the words "full-time" and "part-time", they might have substituted the words "younger" and "older", or "day" and "evening", for that is what they feared.

In its infancy, APUS represented a homogeneous group. A 1969 study of part-time degree students, conducted by

APUS with the co-operation of the Division of Extension, found that two-thirds were married, that 80 per cent of the married students were parents, that half the students were between the ages of 25 and 35 and that another 35 per cent were older than age thirty-five. (*Blyth*, 150) What defined part-time students then, perhaps even more than age and family status, was their employment. Part-time degree students were, by and large, professionals. Almost half were teachers. Another 26 per cent were business people, and six per cent were nurses. The only significant group of non-professionals was the 12 per cent of the part-time population classified as "homemakers".

Percentage of U of T part-time undergraduates (summer and winter) whose first language is neither English nor French: 19

These were the people APUS represented in 1969 when the organization began its crusade for access to the programs and services of the University of Toronto, and, in particular, the Faculty of Arts and Science. Measured by sheer numbers, it appears APUS was successful. With over 13,000 undergraduate and another 2,300 graduate students studying part-time, U of T has more part-time students than any other English language university in Canada. Thirty per cent of its undergraduate students are part-timers. Even more impressive is the growth of its Summer Session, now the largest in North America, in terms of enrolment. Of course, all of this should be weighed against the fact that the University of Toronto is itself Canada's largest university. But for a traditional, research-based institution, U of T has shown remarkable openness to the part-time student.

The growth in enrolment of part-time undergraduate students at U of T is driven by a number of factors, not the least of which was the creation of Woodsworth College in 1974.

However, in the last decade, most of the growth has occurred outside of Woodsworth. This trend suggests that the increase in the number or percentage of part-time students has less to do with a deliberate effort to attract adult learners than with an increase in the numbers of students who might usually study full-time. These students took advantage of the flexibility offered to them through the part-time option. The growing tendency of traditional day students to choose to study at a slower pace was predicted and supported by many in the U of T community who also embraced integration. It has often been argued that all students should be encouraged to study at a pace that makes sense for them, academically and economically. To this end, the growth in part-time study among traditional students should be applauded and is no cause for concern.

The growth in part-time degree student enrolment has certainly not been isolated to the University of Toronto. In fact, Statistics Canada suggested in a 1982 report that part-time degree students stood to become the majority by the year 2000:

> "Based on the authors' predictions of increased part-time participation and a response to the demand thus created, and on the projected age-structure of the Canadian population,

part-time university students could out-number
their full-time counterparts and be 'tomorrow's
majority' on Canadian campuses by the end of
this century." (*Belanger*, 13)

This prediction proved excessively optimistic. In 1994,
with six years left in the century, part-time students
(graduate and undergraduate) are just over a third of the
student body in Canada. For the second year in a
row, part-time enrolment fell nationally, a full six per
cent from 1993.

> **Percentage of U of T part-time undergraduates supported by their employer: 5**

The 1982 Statistics Canada report
pointed to a number of factors which
would affect the enrolment of part-
time degree students, but made the basic assumption that
the terms "part-time" and "adult" were synonymous.
That is, that factors influencing the educational decisions
of Canadians aged 25 to 44, the core part-timers at the
time, would be the most likely indicators of part-time
enrolment trends. In 1982, this assumption made perfect
sense. The average age of part-time students had been
increasing for the past decade; the majority were married;
40 per cent had dependent children. (*Anisef*, ii)

However, the predictions of the early eighties relied on the
continuation of a 20-year trend of increasing interest and
participation in higher education among adults aged 25 to
44. The eighties brought an end to that trend. Between the
years 1981 and 1991, the age composition of the part-time
undergraduate student body in Canada changed

significantly. In 1981, students in the key age range of 30 to 39 years made up 35 percent of part-time undergraduates in Canada. In 1991, they had dropped to 29 per cent. The proportion aged 20 to 24 years had increased by two per cent and the proportion of 40 to 49-year-olds had grown by six per cent. The growth in enrolment of 40 to 49-year-olds can be attributed to the influence of the older baby boomers. This number can be expected to drop as the boomers age. The drop in the proportion of 30 to 39 year-olds is much more difficult to explain.

In the last five years, national university participation rates — the percentage of all Canadians enrolled in university — have grown significantly. The participation

Gross Annual Income of U of T Part-time Students
(includes spousal income for married students)

Under $10,000	20.3%
$10,000 - $19,000	11.4%
$20,000 - $29,999	14.4%
$30,000 - $39,999	15.1%
$40,000 - $49,999	9.4%
$50,000 - $59,000	6.5%
$60,000 or over	17.9%

Source: APUS Student Survey, 1991.

rates of Canadian adults have not. Between 1987 and 1991, the participation rate of 18 to 24-year-olds in part-time undergraduate study grew from 1.3 per cent to 1.7. Participation among 22 to 24-year-olds grew from 3.1 per cent to 3.7. The pattern ends there. In every other age group, the participation rate in part-time undergraduate study has either stayed constant or dropped slightly in the last five years. Full-time programs account for part of the difference. Participation in full-time university study for virtually all age groups has increased in the last five years.

> Percentage of U of T part-time undergraduates who already had a university degree before enroling in current program: 26

For Canadians age 24 and under, the increase was about 2.5 per cent. But for all other age groups, the increase was two-tenths of a percentage point or less. The conclusion is clear: the decline in the number of adult part-time students in Canada is not the result of changes in demographics. And very few have chosen to study full-time instead. The drop in part-time enrolment is due to declining demand among adults.

There is a positive side to this trend. The option of part-time study is becoming increasing popular among young people since it gives them the opportunity to combine school with work or other activities, to continue with their university studies when they might otherwise have dropped out, or to study at a pace more compatible with a physical or learning disability, with parenthood, or with their level of English language proficiency. But the slowly declining participation of adults in university programs is both disconcerting and puzzling, though not inexplicable.

The part-time undergraduate student body at the University of Toronto has changed dramatically since the APUS survey of 1969. In 1991, the Association of Part-time Undergraduate Students decided to examine what was happening with another, more comprehensive, study. APUS distributed over 18,000 surveys, by mail, to the part-time undergraduate students (those registered in fewer than four courses) in the summer and winter sessions of 1991. Over 3,000 students responded to the five-page survey. As a result, more is known about part-time undergraduates at the University of Toronto than at any other institution in Canada.

The 1991 APUS survey revealed that the "typical" part-time student was an outdated notion. Part-time degree

Part-time Undergraduate Enrolment Related to Relevant Age Group

(Percentage of Canadians in each Age Group Enrolled in Part-time Undergraduate Study)

Age	1987-88	1991-92
18-21	1.3	1.7
22-24	3.1	3.7
25-29	2.4	2.4
30-34	2.0	1.8
35-39	1.9	1.7
40-49	1.4	1.4

Source: Statistics Canada: *Education in Canada 1991-92.*

students had become a heterogeneous mass compared to their composition in 1969. In 1991, only one-third were married and more than half the married students had no children. Although the bulk of the students were still in the 25 to 35 age bracket, almost 30 per cent were under 24 years old. And almost a quarter of the students surveyed said that school was their "primary daytime activity." Although most (78 per cent) of the students were employed, less than half had full-time jobs.

Percentage of U of T part-time undergraduates who had a high school diploma or less before enroling in current program: 33

The profile of the summer student had changed most dramatically from the 1960s, when most summer students were teachers back for upgrading. In 1991, the average age of a summer student was just over thirty. Fewer students in the summer were married or had children and more spoke a first language other than English or French. Summer students came from every college of the university, with less than a third from Woodsworth — the traditional source of summer enrolment.

The U of T system gives full- and part-time students access to both day and evening courses. Though it had long been observed that many full-time students were enroled in evening courses, the study revealed that part-time students (almost half) had also crossed the 5:00 p.m. boundary and were taking advantage of the courses available during the day. Although the day students were on average much younger than their evening counterparts, over 60 per cent of the part-time students taking day courses were over the age of twenty-five.

Perhaps the most revealing questions asked in the APUS survey were those concerning students' motivations — why they study and why they study part-time as opposed to full- time. The answers to these questions provide insight into the reasons for both the declining proportion of "typical" part-time students and the increasing interest of younger students in the part-time option.

The survey concluded that the primary motivation among part-time students for pursuing a university education was "to become a better educated person." Across all age groups, the greatest proportion of

> **Percentage of U of T part-time undergraduates whose primary daytime activity is work: 62**

students chose this reason over all others, including the number-two ranked "to increase employment potential." This result should provide some comfort to those in the university who have long worried that universities are becoming mere job training facilities for career-minded students.

Employment is the primary reason students study part-time as opposed to full-time at the University of Toronto. About 30 per cent said they needed to work to cover expenses and another 30 per cent said they wanted to keep a job while studying. Age and other factors played a significant role in responses to this question. As might be expected, more younger students need to work while older students more often said they "wanted to keep a job while studying." (This difference is understandable given that most younger students have yet to embark on a career that gives them a sense of satisfaction.)

Many of the very young students (17 per cent of those under 24) studied part-time only because they had less than four courses left in their degree requirements. Many older students simply preferred the workload of part-time study. Almost 19 per cent of women cited "personal or family responsibilities", compared to less than nine per cent of men.

The 1991 APUS survey confirmed what academics, bureaucrats and students had already observed: part-time and full-time students had become virtually indistinguishable from each other. For the most part, this is a positive development. It rules out the tendency to make generalizations about students based on an arbitrary course load definition of part-time. For APUS, it meant a challenge to its traditional mandate. The organization

---

Reasons Students Study Part-time as Opposed to Full-time
(U of T Arts and Science Degree Students Only)

Need to Work to Cover Expenses	30.8%
Want to Keep a Job While Studying	27.1%
Personal/Family Responsibilities	15.7%
Prefer Workload of Part-time Study	12.4%
Less than 4.0 Courses to Complete Degree	10.2%

Source: APUS Student Survey, 1991.

could no longer serve all, or even the majority, of its membership by concentrating on the concerns of the working adult evening student. Ironically, however, it is this group which most deserves attention, as they are declining in numbers at a time when their increasing participation is thought to be most crucial to Canada's economic well-being.

The blending of young and old, of working and non-working students, of part- and full-timers, in evening, day, winter and summer courses should be viewed as one of the benefits of the integration model. But this benefit must be balanced with the need to protect access for the adult working population for those without the flexibility to choose when they can study. The warning APUS issued in 1971 that traditional full-time students may squeeze part-time students out of their traditional territory of evening and summer courses is still relevant today. But this problem can be met by changes in programming and service operations to reflect the changes in both groups. Two previously distinct types of students are merging to form a large group with compatible needs. This shift represents an opportunity, as well as a challenge, to creative administrators at the University of Toronto.

> **Percentage of UofT part-time undergraduates who took day courses in the Winter Session: 47**

Chapter Three:

OLD HABITS DIE HARD

T wo young students were chatting in the long cafeteria line-up in Sidney Smith Hall one crowded afternoon in early September. "I'm sure I just passed your mom in the hallway upstairs," said one to the other. "What's she doing here?" The other student, oblivious to her friend's disbelief, looked down at her watch and said, "Hey, you're right. She's supposed to be in class right now."

Reactions to presence of adult learners in the classroom at U of T have varied. To some, a range of ages seems more natural, more like what one encounters in the rest of life, and somehow less threatening than facing a sea of young faces. To others, the mature student is a lost cause, a rigid mind incapable of change so late in life. Some see the part-time student as not a "real" student at all, but as someone who takes a few courses in her of his spare time.

Much of the opposition to the integration of part-time students in the early 1970s came in the form of ageism — the tendency to make assumptions about people based on their age rather than on individual ability. The academic abilities of part-time students were pre-judged because they had passed the traditional age for undergraduate education.

One of the committees created to implement the PACE Report of 1970 noted, in a list of inadequacies of the part-time degree program, that, "Old myths persist. It is a widely held belief that part-time students are incapable of producing academic work of a quality comparable to that produced by full-time students." (*Russell*, 5)

> "Outside the immediate environment of Woodsworth College, U of T is a hostile place for part-time students. We frequently remark to each other that we feel penalized for working, for having priorities and responsibilities other than U of T, for being older..."

The Committee then went on to cite studies which had discovered that attendance as a part-time or full-time student had no significant influence on academic achievement where the same academic program and regulations applied to all.

The myth of the academic inferiority of adult students has been exposed and it is now virtually forbidden in academic circles to make such a suggestion. It is still acceptable to claim, however, that the part-time student is too distracted by other responsibilities and activities to be fully engaged in academic life. They are, after all, only partly a student. The evidence that such attitudes still exist are purely anecdotal. There is for example, the recurring story of the U of T history instructor who teaches an evening course and routinely announces sometime during the first lecture of the year that part-time students, particularly those with full-time jobs or other responsibilities during the day, might just as well drop the course. The course is intense, he explains, and is intended for those entirely committed to the concept of being a student, for those without other distractions, for those willing to be fully immersed in the study of history.

Perhaps this instructor believes he is doing his students a favour, warning them of the rigours of the course, in case they enroled with the misguided notion that there would be no homework. However, he is also maintaining the prejudices of an earlier time, when young people either studied or worked, but few did both, and when university studies were a full-time commitment.

In 1993, one-third of Canada's young students (age 15 to 24) worked while attending school full-time. Another 17 per cent were looking for work. For the past twenty-five years, the numbers of young students who work has been steadily increasing, with only the recessions of the early 1980s and 1990s interrupting this trend. (*Sunter*, 34) The challenge of juggling the demands of school and work is no longer exclusive to the older, part-time student.

> "...I find the condescending paternalism of many professors and departments offensive and regressive, and at best an annoying waste of time."
> Woodsworth College, female, age: 32

The Presidential Advisory Committee on Extension at the University of Toronto launched a very frank attack on the groundless distinctions between part-time and full-time students in its 1970 Report:

"The distinction, of course, has traditionally been taken to imply much more than (one who is simply taking fewer courses), mainly on the basis of a set of assumptions which we find ourselves unable to support. One of these is that a student taking what is called a full-time program is necessarily a full-time student in the sense that he devotes all of his time to his studies. That is not only obviously false for virtually all students (and quite properly so), it is not even the case that a majority of students devote a majority of their 'working' hours to their academic work. We must stop pretending that all 'full-time' programmes require full-time effort, and instead deal with the fact that great numbers of full-time programmes can be 'completed' with very partial effort indeed. Another assumption is that the 'other activities' of full-time students are necessarily more valuable than those of part-time students. Yet another has to do with commitment and is related to the first, namely that intellectual commitment is proportional to the number of courses one takes — a full programme implying a full commitment, and less than a full program implying proportionally less commitment. There is so little argument that can be mustered for this assumption that it is difficult to formulate its refutation." (*PACE*, 13)

> "I very much enjoy and respect the friendliness shown to the older students throughout the university."
> Victoria College, female, age: 69

The integration of part-time students into the general curriculum did much to destroy the myths of inferior aptitude and partial commitment among adult, part-time students. In a segregated system, critics of adult education could challenge the integrity of the part-time program, maintaining that its graduates were not worthy of a true

University of Toronto degree. Blending younger and older students, part- and full-time, into the same courses eliminated any doubt that graduates deserved the degrees granted to them.

With the exception of the odd hold-out for the golden days, most faculty members have accepted the presence of the part-time student. However, there remain concerns about the effect part-time study has on the integrity of the programs themselves. These reservations resurfaced in U of T's *Planning for 2000: The Provostial White Paper on University Objectives* released in February 1994: "Concerns have also been expressed about the extent to which part-time study lessens the integrity of programs and the synergy among various courses. (*White Paper*, 35)

> "When my youngest child was in the hospital, I missed classes. I just hope it does not affect my grade and that the teacher will show a little consideration and understanding."
> Erindale College, female, age: 30

Despite these concerns, the prevailing opinion within the central University administration, and the community in general is, as the *White Paper* states, that we should "learn by doing in this area." Indeed, some, including U of T economist and demographer David Foot, suggest that universities will have no choice but to accommodate even more unconventional modes of study as the population of the traditional younger undergraduate clientele shrinks.

Measured against their treatment under the earlier model of "extension" education, part-time students have gained considerably in terms of the respect afforded them within an integrated system. Notions of academic inferiority have been disproved by the academic performance of the students themselves; misconceptions about how dedicated part-time students would be have been erased by changes among the full-time student body; and the value of the degree earned by a part-time student is now beyond reproach since the same degree is awarded to full-time students. With the average age of the full-time undergraduate continually increasing, and the reverse occurring in the part-time population, generalizations about academic performance based on age are no longer credible.

"Part-time engineering students are treated like pariahs by the Department of Engineering. We are constantly hounded to go full-time."
Applied Science and Engineering, male, age: 32.

What barriers of attitude remain, however, are the institutionalized kind that plague many minority groups within the campus. The practices and focus of the University are designed to speak to the majority — the young — with only occasional attention paid to those whose needs and priorities do not fit this mould. Because the University is not yet fully committed to meeting the needs of a diverse body of students, it designs its programs and services to serve the majority, hoping not to offend, too greatly, the rest.

Students are commonly referred to as "kids"; happy, young (though now racially diverse) faces adorn recruitment brochures; and all students are treated as if they just left home for the first time. For older students, these messages are, at best, annoying. At worst, they are an indication of the extent of the change in attitude that is needed to eliminate the barrier of ageism at the University of Toronto.

Chapter Four:

THE PRICE OF LEARNING

A student who began a program in the Faculty of Arts and Science at the University of Toronto in 1984 would have paid about $290 in tuition and incidental fees for one full course. At a rate of two courses per year, that student would be nearing completion of a four-year degree in 1994. In that time, the cost of one course — now over $650 — increased almost two and a half times.

With the inflation levels of the mid-eighties, governments and universities could justify large increases in fees. But tuition and incidental fees have continued to grow, beyond the level of inflation, and well beyond the growth in incomes, which are no longer growing. Ironically, fees rose most sharply through the latest recession, and there is no end to this trend in sight.

Nowhere is the link between income and the cost of education more critical than among the part-time population. According to the 1991 APUS survey, more than 65 per cent of part-time students rely on income from employment as a primary source of funds to cover educational costs. Another 22 per cent depend on their parents, a spouse or their employer. Less than six per cent depend on student assistance programs — in the form of loans, grants or scholarships — which are supplemented to justify each successive tuition fee increase. For part-time students, the problem is not that there is insufficient financial aid doled out to each qualifying student, but that they rarely qualify for any aid to begin with.

"I've had extreme financial difficulties in an attempt to upgrade my education as a single parent. I have borrowed extensively and used all available cash. It is apparent to me that this is the main reason more people do not upgrade their education..."

The patchwork of minor political victories in the area of government financial aid for part-time students is filled with ironies. The Canadian Organization of Part-time University Students (COPUS) was created in the mid-1970s with the objective of convincing the federal Department of the Secretary of State of the injustices of the Canada Student Loans Program. The program remained virtually untouched throughout COPUS's 15-year effort. In the spring of 1994, Lloyd Axworthy, minister of Human Resources Development, (which replaced the Secretary of State), announced long awaited changes to both the full-time and part-time Canada Student Loan programs. By that time, COPUS had deteriorated into a organization with no members, all of them having withdrawn in frustration over the organization's lack of impact at the federal level.

The federal government's 1994 changes were welcomed by APUS, which has attempted to act as a voice for part-time students on the federal scene since the demise of

COPUS. In the context of heightened budget pressures on all levels of government, the cause of the part-time student had garnered sufficient support that the loans program was actually improved. The ceiling on loans was raised from $2,500 to $4,000. But most significant was a change in repayment terms: part-time students had, until the change, been required to begin repaying their loans a month after they borrowed the funds, even though they were presumably still in school. Axworthy gave them relief from repaying the principal — part-time students are now obligated to pay the interest only, until they complete their studies. Ironically, the changes to the part-time program were announced as part of Axworthy's "Youth Employment and Learning Strategy", though these changes will have seemingly little impact on younger students who, by and large, rely on the full-time Canada Student Loan Program. As it turns out, these minor changes to the part-time program were related to the more substantial changes to the full-time program, announced at the same time.

> "...During my first year, I received $4,000 assistance which is very little, especially with two children. I had to sell my house to continue my education."
> Woodsworth College, female, age: 42

Buried in Axworthy's spring 1994 announcements was a change in the eligibility criteria for the full-time CSLP to "emphasize results...by linking student aid to successful and timely completion of studies..." (*HRC Backgrounder*, 10) The program would, beginning in 1995-1996, limit the number of years a student is eligible for loans to the number of years normally required to complete the tudent's program, plus one year. In other words, any student in a four-year degree program who progressed at a rate any slower than four courses per year would exhaust the allotted years of eligibility before completing the degree. This change represents a significant blow to part-time students, particularly the expanding group of students who straddle the arbitrary definitions, fluctuating from part- to full-time, from session to session, according to their personal circumstances. Such fluctuations would no longer be tolerated, at least in the federal aid program. Though the full-time CSL program had always required that students take at least 60 per cent of a full course load in order to qualify, the program had never been concerned with what students did in the years for which they did not qualify. Now students will be relegated to the vastly inferior Part-time Canada Student Loan Program in their final years. This is quite likely the primary rationale for the changes to the part-time program; it was redesigned not to meet the educational needs of the adult labour force but to pick-up the slack for the expensive, youth-oriented, full-time program.

> "The reason I received OSAP one year is because our total income had been practically nothing compared to the previous year. I feel that the financial aid system should be more realistic. It should take account of the bare-bones living for a family."
> Scarborough College, female, age: 37

Unlike its federal counterpart, Ontario's student loan program makes no eligibility distinctions based on course load alone. Ontario has long recognized course load as an artificial and inaccurate means of determining whether a student requires government assistance or not. It has, however, imposed numerous other devices to achieve the same end, that is, to ensure that students complete their programs as quickly as possible and that only the most destitute receive assistance.

In 1993, the Ontario government made an ill-considered attempt to "save now, pay later" by redesigning the Ontario Student Assistance Program (OSAP). By converting the grants portion of a student's award into a "forgivable loan", the NDP government reduced its expenses for the year in which the loan was awarded, and would show the loss later, when the student graduated and the loans were forgiven. Ironically, by eliminating grants, the government had also eliminated two of the program's principal barriers for part-time students. Most part-time students had long been effectively excluded from OSAP's generous grants program because of a time limit on eligibility and a restriction on the amount in assets a student was permitted to own. The assets regulation was clearly designed to eliminate students with a substantial source of wealth; it would force students to sell unnecessary cars or liquidate stocks before they could receive government assistance. What it did, however, was effectively tell adult students to sell their homes before they could be receive any student aid. For many people, selling a home to re-enter the rental market makes very little financial sense. (Although the Ontario government no longer includes assets in their assessment of need, the federal government now plans to introduce them!)

> "Fees for extra-curricular things ie. Hart House, are way too high.
> People who work part-time don't have time to use them but still have to pay for them."
> **Innis College, female, age: 24**

When the grants program disappeared in 1993-1994, so did many of the problems associated with it. What was left was a program seemingly blind to course load or the rate at which a student progressed through their university studies. And accompanying the 1993 changes were two additional bursary programs designed to deal with some of the particular financial barriers many part-time students face. The government sought to enhance access for students with disabilities and students with children by meeting their disability-related and child care costs with bursaries, rather than loans. This program has proven immensely popular, with participation exceeding the government's estimates in its first year.

> "I am a fourth year student who will not complete my degree for at least another two years due to the outrageous extra fees and costs at U of T."
> New College,
> male, age: 23

Apart from these changes, the Ontario student loan program, which is theoretically open to both full- and part-time students, remains youth-focused, providing living expenses at less than social assistance levels to those in the most dire need. The average part-time student, with an income or a supporting spouse, is expected to use those resources to meet their educational costs. Almost 90 per cent of the married students assisted by OSAP in 1993-1994 had a combined family income of under $30,000. Over 60 per cent of married students had a family income under $20,000. Many of these couples were supporting children as well as at least one spouse's educational pursuits. In a period of increasing unemployment and financial hardship, as well as increasing demand for post-secondary education as a means to increasing career choices and prosperity, OSAP funds are targeted toward the most needy, providing larger awards to those with the least resources and greatest expenses. In the meantime, however, the cost of a course or two is being priced out of the reach of the average would-be lifelong learner. Students with a combined spousal income of more than about $30,000, and with educational costs which amount to less than $1,000 are highly unlikely to qualify for OSAP; their relative wealth and low expenses, however, does not mean they have the $650 they need to pay for a course.

In 1975, the Association of Part-time Undergraduate Students, discouraged by its inability to inspire any change to the government-run student aid programs, began to offer

> "Only things such as high tuition fees, book costs and problems getting babysitting at night makes night school less than enjoyable."
> Woodsworth College, female, age: 35

its own bursaries to needy students. Typically, applicants for APUS bursaries need between $500 and $700, and demand always far exceeds the funds available. The number of applications mushrooms in the Summer Session, when almost every other source of bursary funds at the University (with the exception of Woodsworth College) has run dry until the next academic session. The application forms illustrate the diversity of the part-time student population, and the range of situations which the government-run student assistance programs neglect. A refugee claimant supporting a son is ineligible for any government assistance until his claim is accepted. A student's earnings as a part-time computer operator help support his parents, not his education. A newcomer to the province is not yet eligible for Ontario government support but lacks the course load required for the Canada Student Loan Program. A student is abruptly laid-off from her full-time job.

While each story is unique, collectively they represent a failure in the system that becomes particularly acute in times of economic decline or upheaval. Means-tested student aid programs simply cannot accommodate the range of personal and economic tragedies, responsibilities, and occasional misjudgments that typify the part-time population.

"I didn't apply for OSAP because I assumed I wouldn't be eligible. I'm single, work full-time and own a condo. I'm pretty sure this would mean I'm not eligible." Scarborough College, female, age: 26

It is tempting to suggest that since it is the cost of the courses themselves which presents the most significant barrier to the part-time student, or at least to those ill-served by the current aid programs, that reducing or eliminating tuition fees is the appropriate solution. Aside from being politically impractical, increasing the public subsidy to university students in this way would exacerbate an already regressive situation: taxpayers would be required to pay more to subsidize a group that, after graduation, will include the nation's most economically advantaged citizens. And, in fact, there is a significant proportion of the part-time population which is already relatively wealthy — almost 18 per cent of respondents to the 1991 APUS survey reported an combined spousal income of $60,000 or more.

In 1993, APUS, along with other members of the Ontario Undergraduate Student Alliance, proposed a practical solution to the dilemma of rising fees and declining aid.

Full and part-time students, it claimed, needed only to be able to write-off the costs of courses (and living expenses in some cases) against their future earnings. If those earnings failed to reach a level at which the debt could reasonably be repaid, then, and only then, would the public subsidy kick in.

The plan — called income-contingent loan repayment — had been advocated by others in the past, though rarely as a solution to the needs of part-time students. The plan has even greater appeal when applied to part-time students than to their full-time counterparts. For students, it provides both access to government loans without the government's intrusive and frequently absurd means-testing system, as well as a guarantee that the repayment terms will be manageable. For government, the plan offers a low-cost method of providing assistance to a group of students critical to maintaining a highly educated labour force, a group whose years of work experience and post-secondary education make them a particularly low-risk investment.

> "Part-time students can take many years to complete their studies. Because of this, an escalating burden may exist, in part due to ongoing inflation over many years. Why, then, are we often denied discounts and services that are exclusive to full-time students? I am currently in my seventh course and cannot claim any of them on my income tax return because they have been taken one at a time. Disgraceful!"
> Woodsworth College, male, age: 43

The stability of the plan depends upon tuition fee levels being kept within a range which the average graduate will be able to repay in a reasonable time frame. To ensure this, fee increases would be tied to inflation. This security would allow those entering the system on one set of assumptions about the cost of their program to predict, with reasonable certainty, their final debt.

The income-contingent loan plan enjoyed the political support of the NDP government, not because of its particular appeal in assisting part-time learners, but because the existing aid program, has been recognized as inequitable and inefficient. At the federal level, income-contingent loans were proposed most recently by Human Resources Minister Axworthy as a method by which the costs of post-secondary education could be transferred from governments to students. His plan was later shelved. Though various groups who opposed his plan take credit for having convinced him to withdraw it, it is more likely that the federal government eventually realized the essential flaw in the plan; income-contingent loans cannot be used to accommodate large tuition increases, as the plan's stability depends entirely on manageable debts for the average student. Axworthy's plan failed to recognize this relationship. It is, however, possible to design a workable student aid program using the principles of income-contingency when the objective is to create a fair system and eliminate some of the flaws of the current system. In doing so, governments have the opportunity to create all-encompassing programs which meet the needs of both part- and full-time students, who are, in most other respects, indistinguishable.

There is, however, a particular group of potential students who will be ill-served by any loans program, and they are

> "In order to qualify for any financial assistance, I'd have to be bankrupt. As I am entirely self-supporting, with no parental or spousal support, I can't go to school full-time. It is impossible."

beginning to garner some attention. Older unemployed workers pursuing university education as a route back into the labour force are better suited to full-time study than to part-time study. Part-time study merely serves to prolong their period of unemployment. With a shorter pay-off period remaining in their working life, these students would be unlikely to be able to repay substantial loans and, indeed, it would be unwise to make such an investment. These students need access to non-repayable funds to maintain an appropriate standard of living for themselves and their families and to allow them to complete their programs as quickly as possible.

Canada's existing income support programs, such as unemployment insurance or social assistance benefits, could serve this purpose. This change, to provide incentives for older workers to pursue education as a means to employment and self-sufficiency, would require substantial political will and faith that the university system can fulfil that role.

Chapter Five:

THE LONG HAUL

I t is foolish to make generalizations about such a diverse lot as adult part-time students, but if there is one thing they have in common, it is probably fatigue. The evening student typically spends one or two nights a week on campus — rushing from work, missing dinner with the family, facing a long trip home at 9 or 10 p.m. — for a seemingly endless number of years. They take their study time whenever they can find it: during lunch hour, late at night, or on weekends. While most persist, many do not. The reasons, of course, are as diverse as the students themselves. Some of the factors which make adult learners give up have little to do with the University: a change in priorities, a new job, a move out of commuting distance. Much of what conquers the part-time student — or more precisely the evening and summer student — is the structure of the academic program itself.

In preparation for the integration of part-time students in 1972, the Faculty of Arts and Science formed a committee, chaired by constitutional scholar Peter Russell, to provide advice on the improvement of the part-time degree program. One of the many practical issues the Russell

Committee considered was the appropriate range of courses to be available during the evening and summer. It concluded that, "Each Department (should) plan its offerings in winter evening and summer sessions in such a way that each course is normally available outside the 9-4 weekday hours at least once every three years." (*Russell, 7*)

Many of the committee's recommendations were subsequently ignored, but the abandonment of this particular principle would create the most frustration for the part-time student. The University of Toronto offers over an impressive array of evening arts and science courses — over 300 full course equivalents in 50 areas of study during the winter on the St. George Campus alone. The list of courses has remained relatively stable, even over periods of general cost-cutting at the University. Adult learners have a selection of evening and summer courses which includes some taught by high profile and respected ˙faculty members like Professor Michael Bliss of the History Department and Professor Mel Watkins of the Department of Economics. Largely due to the work of staff at Woodsworth College who co-ordinate the course list, evening students have access to a part of what makes U of T an exceptional institution — its outstanding faculty.

> **"Course scheduling must be handled by the school of Medieval Studies. Courses should be over in four months. Modern life is too fast. People need the flexibility to take courses when and if they can...."**
> **Woodsworth College, male, age: 37**

Only after several years of attending evening classes does the promise fade and the frustration emerge, as the limitations of the course list become a serious obstacle to completing a program of study.

Many of the Faculty of Arts and Science's courses are virtual fixtures on the evening course timetable, but many important courses are not. Whether a course will be offered to evening students largely depends on whether an instructor is willing to teach it in the evening. As a result, those faculty members who like to teach in the evening — and many prefer evening courses because of the presence of more adults in the classroom — do it on a regular basis. In fact, it becomes obvious when an instructor has gone on sabbatical, as the course he or she regularly teaches in the evening will suddenly disappear from the timetable in a particular year, only to reappear when the instructor returns.

> "... This idea that a course should only be offered once a year, in September in the day, is only sensible in an agrarian society, not in a modern urban one. Every fall we see thousands of students falter, and if they blow the first few weeks, they have to wait a whole year to try again, or try something else. Sadistic and senseless."
> Woodsworth College, male, age: 37

The problem is not the predictability of when the courses will be offered. In fact, this system has its advantages. It has often been suggested that part-time students would benefit from an "advance" timetable, displaying the evening and summer course offerings for the next three years, so that students could plan their academic progress accordingly. The problem is the number of courses, especially in some departments and most acutely within the third and fourth years of a program. The Department of Economics, to take a typical example, has offered the same four third year courses since 1987-1988, with the addition of one or two extras in alternating years. In that time, it has never offered any fourth year courses in the evening. By contrast, it offers over two dozen third year and one dozen fourth year courses during the day.

With such limited numbers of courses, departments put the evening student in a perilous position. With a couple of retirements, completing a program through evening study could become impossible.

The University of Toronto offers both a three-year and four-year degree. The future of the three-year degree is in question and has been the focus of some debate. In essence, the battle is about the relative value of quality and access. Members of the University concerned about the integrity of a degree requiring only three years (15 courses) of study want it abolished. Members of the University concerned that, for many students, the option of a three-year degree means the difference between completing and dropping-out want to keep it. The primary opponents to the elimination of the three-year degree have been Woodsworth College and APUS.

"It's very difficult to complete an undergrad degree at U of T on a part-time basis. As for courses I am interested in, it's ridiculous. The only reason I am not taking a course this semester is that I could find one on either the Erindale or St. George Campus."
Erindale College, female, age: 33

The 1991 APUS Survey found some significant differences among students intending to complete a three-year degree and those prepared to complete the longer four-year program. Women are more likely to opt for the shorter degree, as are older students, parents, and evening students. Especially revealing is the relationship between the desire to complete a four-year degree and the level at which the student is currently studying. While only a third of first-year students said they intended to complete a three-year degree, almost 60 per cent of third-year students saw the end in sight and were planning to stop at a three-year degree. This data tells the story of the exhausting experience many part-time degree students encounter. Students embark on programs eager for the long haul; they end-up tired and disappointed, ready to forsake their original goals for the short term satisfaction of having received a degree. The best solution is not to eliminate the three-year degree but to eliminate the barriers to earning a four-year degree. The University has accepted this challenge by leaving the question open and pledging to study the alternatives.

The 1991 APUS Survey found that almost 30 per cent of part-time students were either somewhat or highly dissatisfied with the availability and/or timing of courses required for their program. A third of the students were dissatisfied with the availability of courses which interested them, but which may not have been required for their program. The highest levels of dissatisfaction were found among students in the 35 to 44 age group, among those who worked, and among those in the upper years of their programs. Very high levels of dissatisfaction with course selection were found among students at both the Erindale and Scarborough campuses. Not at all coincidentally, students at the suburban campuses were much more likely to be planning to complete only a three-year degree. Students at both of these campuses ranked "evening course selection" as the most pressing problem

"I am currently enroled in fourth year. I need two more Psych credits after completing my current course. It is going to take me three years to get these credits because of the scheduling of the particular courses I require.... I do find this frustrating and very costly time-wise for my career ambitions."
Woodsworth College, female, age: 34

at the University — well above underfunding of the university, large class sizes, quality of instruction, financial aid and a number of other pressing issues.

None of this surprises administrators and faculty at Scarborough College where departments are small and evening courses are waning in number. In the summer of 1993, the College established a Task Force to look at this problem. Its conclusion: tell students the truth about which programs can realistically be completed through evening and summer study. In fact, Scarborough has long been forthright about what it can and cannot offer to the student who works during the day. When it becomes obvious that a program simply cannot be completed through evening and summer study, it is simply deleted from the list of such programs in the Scarborough College calendar. Scarborough still offers eight programs of study to the evening student, although the Sociology major and specialist programs have recently disappeared from the list.

> "As someone working full-time in a position which frequently makes evening meetings mandatory, Saturday classes would be a great asset in diminishing fatigue, and thus enhancing active participation."
> St. Michael's College, male, age: 48

For many part-time students, Summer Session represents a kind of academic paradise. The campus is teeming with adult students. The instructors of summer courses assume that most of their students work. The courses are over in three months.

The University of Toronto has the largest Summer Session in North America, with about 16,000 students and over

300 courses spread over three campuses. (*White Paper*, 35) But there is trouble in this paradise. The number of courses offered is not keeping pace with the rapid increases in enrolment. Since 1987, enrolment in U of T's Summer Session has increased by 44 per cent. In the same period, the course timetable grew by only 10 per cent. The result: courses fill-up quickly, seemingly immediately. Others have huge enrolments. In the past, these have been Winter Session problems, but they are now plaguing summer students as well.

Nowhere is the problem more acute than at Erindale College. Since 1987, summer enrolment at Erindale has grown almost 50 per cent to about 3,000 students. In the same period, the course

> **"Finishing an Anthropology degree at night is very difficult as most 300 and 400 level courses are held in the daytime."**
> Victoria College,
> female, age: 36

list has shrunk by 27 per cent to only 46 full course equivalents. The list is now so short it can be read out by a machine over the telephone to inquiring students.

At least part of the summer enrolment growth at all campuses of U of T is made up of students from other universities. Unlike U of T, many other Ontario universities are left vacant and virtually unused for the summer months. And since many of these students' parents live in Toronto, they find it both economical and convenient to move home for the summer and pick up extra credits through U of T. This would be a perfectly tolerable situation if U of T were able to meet this demand. But adding courses to the summer timetable at U of T is a financial issue: the instructors who teach summer courses at U of T are paid a stipend, whether they are regular full-time faculty or contract teachers. Each course represents an additional stipend. Although advocates of expanded summer course offerings suggest integrating summer courses into the regular teaching load of full-time faculty, this change is unlikely to be welcomed by the faculty members themselves who are used to having the summer months for research or other purposes. The effect is twofold: fewer summer courses are taught by full-time faculty members, who may not necessarily be superior teachers but can provide students with consistent contact, a connection with the department and a glimpse into the research side of the University — all things an undergraduate deserves. Second, the selection of summer courses is highly dependent on budgets, and cannot expand without funding. At Erindale, the result is a much reduced list. When there are fewer courses to choose from, this only serves to make a long haul even longer for part-time students.

> "In order to achieve my academic goals...I will have to switch to full-time studies for third and fourth year. Dependent on where I am positioned in my career objectives, I may have to forgo my dream of obtaining a university degree. Course availability seems aimed at an elite that can pick and choose their working hours. More Saturday and evening choices would be great!"
> Woodsworth College, female, age: 34

Though night and summer school have been the prevailing methods of delivering degree courses to adult learners, there are alternatives. U of T has made some attempts at other modes of course delivery, but it is hardly a leader in this respect. Innovation in the delivery of undergraduate courses to adult students has met with limited success. Off-campus courses, in office buildings, shopping malls and libraries, existed in the 1970s, but have long since been cancelled for financial reasons. The majority of arts and science courses at U of T are still "full-year" courses running from September to April.

For many part-time students, this is simply too long a period to devote one or two evenings a week to attending classes. Although the 1991 APUS Survey revealed that some 60 per cent of part-time students would take a Saturday course if one was offered in their field, in 1994-1995 only six courses were offered on weekends. Distance education is virtually unheard of at U of T, especially in Arts and Science. Beyond the Faculty of Arts and Science,

> "I would like to see more night time courses offered at Scarborough.
> Too many of them are located downtown."
> **Scarborough College,**
> female, age: 32

the opportunities for part-time study are few and far between. There are some professional programs — nursing, applied science and engineering — which allow students to study at a rate suitable for them, but many do not.

APUS lobbied extensively in the mid-eighties for the creation of a part-time program in the Faculty of Law. It achieved what is called "half-time" law, an option available only to students whose personal circumstances simply do not allow them to study full-time. The criteria are so rigid that having a full-time job does not count as a reason for studying part-time. As a result, there are fewer than ten students registered in this program.

The resistance to part-time study in professional faculties is not based primarily on financial limitations. Launching an evening program is an expensive endeavour if it involves the duplication of course offerings. However, creating a part-time option with the courses already offered, and simply allowing students to study at a pace convenient to them, has fewer financial implications. The reluctance to allow this option is normally rooted in two notions. The intensity of the experience and the interdependency of the courses are cited as reasons for insisting on full-time study. Of course, this argument was employed by the opponents of integration in the Faculty of Arts and Science 25 years ago. The other argument used is that the program is already receiving more than enough qualified applicants willing to study full-time; there is no need to serve a whole other clientele. Administrators and faculty who use this argument to restrict part-time students are only denying themselves the opportunity to admit and teach some of the most worthy students.

> "The most important issue with me is the availability of required courses. There's no reason for required ones to be offered during the day. I am currently taking a Saturday course. I think it would be great if more were offered so I could avoid downtown driving and parking by taking more than one per day."
> Innis College,
> female, age: 24

There are signs that the University of Toronto is trying to become more responsive to the adult student. Most notably, the Provostial *White Paper* released in February 1994 recommended that:

> "Experimentation with different schedules and formats for undergraduate education should be encouraged, including the offering of courses

in intensive modules, improvement of the Summer Session, work-study programs and more frequent scheduling of courses on evenings and weekends."(*White Paper*, 35)

This recommendation not only represents a radical shift in the respect and attention afforded to adult study, but suggests that the central administration is ready to lead the University through the kinds of changes and challenges necessary to play its role in the lifelong learning society. This is a role that many administrators and faculty have, until now, seen little reason to assume. It seems the University of Toronto feels it no longer has a choice. The *White Paper*'s rationale for this change is that "the number of students pursuing their programs while balancing other respon-

> "I was very excited to find out that the University was offering part-time courses toward a law degree. I was then disappointed that it only applies to students who have a reason (financial or handicapped) for attending part-time. Although I am neither of those, I would not be able to return to full-time study for three years and would like the opportunity to go to law school on a part-time basis."
> Woodsworth College, female, age: 26

sibilities will increase, if the pattern of 'life-long learning' foreseen by education policy analysts continues to develop." (*White Paper*, 34-35) But lifelong learning will not continue to develop unless and until universities create the environment to foster it. If the University of Toronto and other universities change their routines to accommodate adult learners, lifelong learning will flourish. But universities can easily choose to resist the demands for adult education, by reinforcing the walls around the fortress, ignoring the needs of adults and conducting business as usual.

It would be easy to understand why the University of
Toronto might want to avoid leading the charge to
innovation in adult education. In comparison with other
universities, it is already leading the way in providing
opportunities for adults — at least in the on-campus
format. If its enthusiasm is subsiding after 20 years of
effort, it is mainly due to a decade of underfunding. To
begin the kind of innovation needed to truly accommodate the adult workforce would require political commitment from the highest levels of the
University, as well as partners from
outside.

> "As a part-time student, and
> a full-time employee, I don't
> seem to find any courses
> given after 5 p.m. that are
> towards my major (math).
> I'm starting to get
> discouraged."
> Erindale College,
> female, age: 25

Throughout U of T's quarter century
experiment with part-time study, it has
received negligible support from the
sector which should serve as a full part-
ner in the race toward a society of lifelong learning — the
Canadian business community.

Universities cannot bear the sole responsibility for creating an environment where lifelong learning does not
mean lifelong sacrifice. Students must also be prepared for
the challenge. Degree study is the most intense and
difficult form of education an adult can attempt. Yet part-
time students are clearly willing to take on this challenge.
What frustrates them are the unnecessary barriers to what
they can clearly see would be a smoother learning path; a
path that includes the courses that interest them as well as
the ones they need; a path that provides them flexibility
when circumstances change; a path that affords them the
same quality in classroom experience as their day and full-
time counterparts.

Beyond the commitment of the students, the university and governments, lifelong learning, to become as pervasive as we need it to be, requires the co-operation of the public and private sector employers whose workers are toiling away in libraries and classrooms, night after night, unsupported by their employers who will ultimately share in the benefits of this effort. Perhaps the best way employers can support the educational endeavours of their employees is not simply to cover tuition costs, but to provide time.

The promises, throughout the seventies and eighties, of a four-day work week, less overtime, and more leisure time have never materialized. And although "training" has long been integrated into the work week, higher education has not. Education is still perceived as a personal endeavour with personal rewards. But in the emerging knowledge-based economy, higher education is the most valuable form of training on the market. Employers, by and large, have yet to recognize this new reality. Though they will sponsor employees to acquire a new technical skill, they are reluctant to provide them with the time and support to understand a foreign culture, or to explore a scientific theory. With the participation of employers, the possibilities for innovation in delivering courses are endless. Without it, new ideas in course formats run the risk of empty classrooms, with employees unable to participate because of inflexible employers. In the meantime, education will remain a private activity and universities may only be able to tinker with the system to make the long haul a little shorter.

Chapter Six:

A DIFFERENT SET OF NEEDS

I t is a Thursday night in early December, 1993, and a crowd of about a hundred people has gathered in one of Hart House's most charming rooms to celebrate the achievements of some extraordinary students. As each name is called, a student emerges, crosses a creaky wooden floor and receives an award from APUS President Nancy Watson. The crowd begins to murmur after about the fifth name. By the eighteenth and final name, everyone has noticed the same thing. Almost all of the scholarship winners are women, the youngest probably in her mid-thirties, the oldest in about her mid-fifties. Some have brought their families to celebrate with them. And though they are different in many ways, they have one thing in common, besides gender — an enviable grade point average.

None of this surprises people who work with part-time students at U of T on a day-to-day basis. Over 60 per cent of part-time students are female and the proportion is much higher among older students. According to the 1991 APUS Survey, women made up 77 per cent of part-time students between the ages of 35 and 44 and over 80 per cent of those aged 45 to 54. About a quarter of female part-time students have children. For many of these people the option of part-time study represents a sec ond chance at a university education. With the demands of home and family taking precedence in their younger years, they have returned to seize the opportunity to get an education on a part-time basis. They are among the most serious and committed of students at U of T.

"Although I would like to use the various facilities and services available, my full-time job and part-time studies don't leave me enough time to do so...."
Woodsworth College
female, age: 32

These are the kinds of students the University of Toronto wants and indeed needs, to attract, according to the Provost's 1994 *White Paper: Planning for 2000*. Although it is not entirely clear how the University will attract more students with career and family obligations, the *White Paper* recognizes explicitly the benefits of having a mature, yet academically eager, component to the student body. And to a large degree, although not entirely smoothly, the academic programs of the University have been adjusted to accommodate these students through the provision of evening and summer courses and the creation of Woodsworth College. That was the easy part. Programs are merely conglomerations of courses and there is much more to "student life" than that. The true story of the U of T integration experiment has yet to be written as part-time and adult students continue to be welcomed in theory, but in practice, are excluded from important aspects of the student experience.

Like most universities, the University of Toronto takes a holistic approach to the treatment of its students. The student is seen not merely as a person who studies, but as a person with health care, housing, social, employment, financial and other personal needs which are all related to the overall success of the student. When these other needs are not met, the student's ability to succeed is jeopardized. This is why the University takes an interest in the so-called non-academic needs of its students. By providing a medical and psychiatric clinic for students, recreational centres, student residences and a housing placement service, an employment counselling and job placement service and a multitude of social organizations designed to foster collegiality and friendship, the University helps reduce the barriers to success. Most of these services are centralized (with the exception of the Scarborough and Erindale campuses which have their own units) and, in almost all cases, part-time students are permitted to use them. Few, however, do.

> "... I would like to be given a choice of using these facilities/services and paying non-academic fees for some or not using them and not paying the fee. (Almost a third of my tuition goes to support facilities and services I never get the opportunity to use!"
> Woodsworth College, female, age: 32

The infrastructure of student services at the University is oblivious to age and personal circumstance. On the positive side, this open-door policy means the services are available to part-time students, regardless of their course loads. But while the doors may be open to part-time and adult students (although many of the service units have few, if any, evening hours), the services inside are designed to meet the needs of the traditional university clientele — youth. Since young people still far outnumber adult students on each campus, the services can hardly be blamed for maintaining their youth-oriented focus. However, there is no parallel set of services designed to deal with the needs of older students. And these inequities are aggravated by the fact that student fees are the source of funding for most of these services, including the hard-earned money of part-time students.

> "I do not see why I should have to pay for services I do not use and I know other students who feel the same way."
> Woodsworth College, male, age: 22

The 1991 APUS Survey found that part-time students' use of most campus services decreased as their age increased. Although no single service was used by more than 30 per cent of the part-time student population, use was even lower among older students. The reasons are obvious. First, adult students come to university with an established network of off-campus support and services. The vast majority already have a family physician, a job, a home, and friends, and use the recreational facilities near home or work. Second, what they need from the University is not available to them. Although all students have access to the Career Centre's part-time and temporary job postings, (most offering low hourly wages), the permanent salaried jobs are restricted to those who have graduated or are about to graduate, regardless of work experience. (The rationale for this restriction is that employers specify that they want applications limited to those with a degree.)

Student family housing is provided only to full-time students, with the exception of single parents. Most of the campus is child-unfriendly, including the recreational facilities. Evening hours for many of the services are limited to one night a week. Weekend hours are unheard of, with the commendable exception of recreational facilities.

As a result of a series of decisions in the early 1990s, all student services at the University of Toronto are funded almost exclusively by student fees. In 1994-1995, each part-time student on the St. George Campus paid over $115 to support campus services like these. If they return in the Summer Session, they will pay this amount again. And the fees are scheduled to rise again in 1995-1996.

> "I would like to see administration offices and services have hours which are more convenient to night students. I'm finding it difficult at present to clear up a fee problem because of the hours of the fees office."
> Innis College, female, age: 26

The lack of appropriate and accessible services for adult students is not a recent discovery. The President's Advisory Committee on Extension called attention to the problem in its 1970 Report:

> "The University must become more seriously concerned with the various kinds of counselling required by all students ... In particular, there must be a realistic assumption of responsibility for part-time student welfare and an improvement in the professional services that psychologists, counsellors and advisers, and others provide." (*PACE*, 17)

The report specifically identified the health centre and career counselling as services which would need to adjust to the integration of part-time students. Almost 25 years later, not only have many of the existing services failed to make the necessary adjustments, only one new service has emerged which meets the distinct needs of adult students.

The exception is child care. The 1990s have seen small and symbolic improvements in the University's support for students with children. Many people are surprised to learn that there are an estimated 4,000 part-time under-graduate students at U of T who are supporting children. This seems like a lot for a university where one rarely sees children. But compared to the propor-tion of adults in the general population who have children, the number of parents among the adult student popu-lation at U of T is disproportionately low. Parents, especially those of young children, are staying away from campus. Not only are adults waiting until their children are in school before they make the plunge back into formal learning, but many students who have children mid-way through their studies are not completing their degrees. This is a long-standing problem which should have been solved by more liberal attitudes toward child care. Instead, students are prevented from participating in higher education because of a lack of affordable care for their children.

> "It is absolutely unbelievable that a university that offers part-time studies cannot get the time slot for photo ID's sooner than October 21. Come on Woodsworth, you have more pull than this! Show support for part-timers and get services scheduled at night too."
> Woodsworth College, female, age: 33

The early years of child's life should be an ideal time for a parent to study at a university. Parents who have given up all or part of an income to stay home with their children should be able to participate in higher education on a part-time basis. Unfortunately, the design of the child care system works against this option. Part-time students do not require full-time care for their children; in fact, even many full-time students require less than full-time, 9 a.m. to 5 p.m. daily care for their children. But part-time care in a government-regulated, non-profit form is almost non-existent in the Toronto area. Some child care centres permit half-time enrolment but only in a form — five mornings or five afternoons per week — which rarely meets the requirements of a student's course timetable. The only other alternatives for students are usually too expensive to be considered options at all, such as full-time care or a babysitter hired on an hourly basis.

> "The cost of daycare is ridiculous if you don't have subsidy and there is no part-time available."
> Scarborough College, female, age: 28

Some universities, such as York and the University of Western Ontario, are beginning to fill this void with the creation of child care centres designed to serve the unique needs of students. The University of Toronto has two such centres. The first, established at Erindale College in 1992, started small by caring for only five children at a time and has since tripled its capacity. The second, opened on the St. George Campus in 1993, offers care for 15 children at a time and its available spaces were filled at peak hours before it even opened its doors. It is currently seeking a larger space.

The concept of part-time child care seems only natural to the parents who need it, but is virtually revolutionary to the child care sector. The Provincial government has been hesitant to license such unconventional programs and will not provide them with funding.

Municipal governments refuse to provide subsidies to the parents, though they subsidize the fees for full-time care. Part-time child care requires much greater administrative costs as scheduling changes according to the class and study timetables of the parents and vacancies during particular hours of the day are a fact of life. In spite of these obstacles, interest in this kind of facility is growing and new centres at other campuses are being developed, often initiated by students themselves.

"When one works full-time and takes courses part-time, who has the time for all the other amenities we pay for in our fees— such as the Athletic Centre. That fee should be 'pay as you use'."
Woodsworth College, female, age: 27

There is much more to be done to facilitate university study for the parents of young children and others whose family responsibilities impede their access. In the fall of 1993, the University of Toronto created a new position of Family Care Advisor, a person charged with assisting students in balancing their study and family responsibilities. Overworked and limited to spending only half her time helping students, (the other half is spent with staff and faculty — a peculiarity resulting from a unique funding arrangement), the Family Care Advisor provides information on everything from finding a suitable child or elder care program to dealing with OSAP. Her job is a frustrating one. For every bandage she applies to a student in need, there is a gaping wound in the system that could be healed with co-ordination between the various bureaucracies with which a student deals. But in a period in which student services rarely expand, and, when they do, affect the cost of education directly, students are lucky to have the services of even a half-time worker.

Many adult students want nothing more from the University of Toronto than a great lecturer, a desk to sit at and access to the library. They complain bitterly that the University is over-charging them for services and facilities they will never use. When the position of Family Care Advisor was created, the only signifi-cant opposition to it came from the Graduate Students' Union which said the University was duplicating services already available in the external community. The graduates had a legitimate point: if students are attached to their home communities more than they are to their campus, they should not have to pay for services they have no intention of using.

> "Part-time daycare for newborns and up should be made available. If I am tak-ing a class twice a week for a couple of hours, I require child care."
> Woodsworth College, female, age: 33

Time is precious for most part-time students and even for many full-time students who commute to campus, hold down part-time jobs and have a social life centred elsewhere. Many U of T students are on campus as little as possible, often only to attend classes. This reality contra-dicts the traditional notion that university is the centre of every student's existence, and that campus life is an integral part of the educational experience of a university. It may no longer be realistic to regard student life as mandatory, rather than optional. Student organizations have begun to realize this and have created "opt-out" provisions in their fee structures for services like health insurance. Perhaps it is time for the University to follow suit.

The University of Toronto can barely afford to provide the adult, part-time, evening student with access to the services which are vital to a university education. Woodsworth College, though it is hardly the only college with evening students, is the only one which has regular evening hours for its Registrar's Office. During the Summer Session, colleges other than Woodsworth provide abysmal academic service, closing computer labs and libraries and offering none of their regular bursaries, despite the presence of hundreds of their students on campus. The suburban campuses of Scarborough and Erindale, where thou-

> "I am expecting a baby in January. I would like to see more infant and toddler daycare."
> Woodsworth College, female, age: 27

sands of part-time students are registered, provide even fewer evening and summer services. The days of the 24-hour library are long gone and reference and other services are increasingly restricting, rather than expanding, hours of operation. Until the early 1990s, Sidney Smith Hall, the St. George Campus's main undergraduate academic building, was not equipped with a wheelchair ramp. Many other buildings remain inaccessible to students with physical disabilities and most recent improvements have been funded through a fee full-time students chose to impose on themselves.

All of this speaks to the need, now greater than ever, for a college which serves part-time and adult students as its primary clients — a staff equipped to deal with their needs, a wheelchair accessible building, hours of service that reflect the reality of students' busy lives. The St. George Campus has all this in Woodsworth College. But

the presence of Woodsworth does not mean that the rest of
the University can abdicate its responsibilities to meet the
needs of lifelong learners. This is especially true at the
suburban campuses, where students can not be steered
toward Woodsworth because the suburban college feels
ill-equipped to serve them.

The role and purpose of the college structure at the
University of Toronto has been a subject of constant
debate. To many, the duplication of services seems wasteful in a time of budget
restraint. Others point out that central-
ization will exacerbate the sense of
bureaucratization and alienation that
plague the St. George Campus. The role

> "Evening instruction for use
> of library facilities is needed
> forpart-time students. Using
> Robarts for research can be
> difficult if students are
> unsure of the services."
> Woodsworth College,
> female, age: 30

of Woodsworth has never been more clear. Woodsworth
does for its adult students what the rest of the University
cannot or will not do. But the College does not, and likely
never will, have the resources to provide all of the services
and support needed by all of the adult learners in the
University. It is already the largest college in the
University, and has been since its creation. It has also
assumed the role of an advocate for the interests of part-
time students beyond the college walls. Woodsworth is a
small, but essential part of the University for most adult
learners; it cannot become the only division in the
University committed to creating an environment to
support lifelong learning. It needs help.

The provision of services to adult and part-time students
should be seen as an equity measure which the entire

University has a responsibility to fulfil. It makes little
difference for Woodsworth College to have a wheelchair
ramp and electronic doors, if the libraries and other
essential buildings do not offer similar access. A part-time
child care centre on the St. George or Erindale Campus
does not help a parent at Scarborough. The evening atten-
dant at the New College Registrar's Office cannot
provide information to a Trinity College student who
works all day. In a climate of cuts, rather than expansion,
the University is unlikely to be able to create a more
equitable campus. But it should at least consider the
question and approach the issue honestly, rather than
avoid it by maintaining that its open-door policy for
student services meets the needs of part-time and adult
students.

Conclusion:

A LEARNING EXPERIENCE

F or the second year in a row, part-time enrolment at Canadian universities fell in 1994. Initially, administrators were baffled. Some said a turnaround in the economy had tempted students back into the workforce, rather than into universities. A vice-president at York University, which experienced an 11 per cent drop in part-time students in 1994, told *The Globe and Mail* that, "The demand wasn't there." (November 22, 1994, p. A4) At Acadia University, where part-time enrolment dropped a staggering 23 per cent, the registrar told *University Affairs*, "We were wondering ourselves where they went to." (December 1994, p. 48)

Part-time students did not suddenly choose to leave Canadian universities. The past decade has seen only slight growth in part-time enrolment, inflated by the educational pursuits of the baby boom. The next generation of potential adult learners shows less and less inclination to enter university. Statistics Canada's records of participation rates demonstrate a trend toward decreasing interest in part-time study among adults.

Various explanations were bandied about when the reports of a drop in part-time enrolment hit the media. The most popular rationale was that a growing economy had drawn students back into the workforce. Viewed this way, a drop in enrolment could be seen as a positive trend. However, the part-time student population has always been made up primarily of people who were already working. An increase in employment should have little effect on their decisions about education, particularly when lifelong learning is seen to be of such importance to future success in the world of work.

While administrators and policy-makers wonder what is luring part-time students away from universities, an obvious explanation is being overlooked. Policy-makers project that, eventually, adults will be forced back to school by a restructured economy that requires a work-force of lifelong learners. But like a baseball diamond in the middle of a cornfield, universities must learn that only "if you build it, they will come." Students are not being lured away from universities, they are being driven away by an educational system which continually frustrates them. And they will only be lured back when the system is rebuilt.

In its August 1994 discussion paper on funding the province's university system, the Ontario Council on University Affairs predicted a "growing demand for life-long learning" (*OCUA*, 5) as one of the factors affecting future enrolment.

The cause of this demand:

"Given the profound restructuring of the economy, it is highly likely that there will be a growing demand for a 'quilt-like' combination of education in its broadest sense that will involve learning and training provided by universities, colleges and private corporations." (*OCUA*, 5)

In other words, economic necessity will force adults to return to school. The key question is: where will they go? To a community college, where the programs are more economical, compact and professionally-oriented? To private training programs which cater explicitly to the adult worker? Or to the universities, where the programs are costly, time-consuming, and designed primarily to meet the needs of youth?

Universities stand to miss out on the anticipated resurgence in adult education if they do not adapt. The result would not only be a great loss to the potential students, but a loss to the Canadian economy as a whole. It has become increasingly evident that a university degree, in any discipline, is not only relevant in the job market, but is the key to prosperity in the job market of the future. The university degree demonstrates a level of adaptability and ingenuity that is essential to the knowledge-based economy. The value of the university degree has been confirmed by unemployment rates throughout the recession of the early 1990s; the university-educated suffered the least of any group during that period, when jobs for those with a university degree actually increased. Though the idea persists, through the popular media that the university-educated suffered through the recession, the evidence points to the opposite.

If universities want to fulfil their role in the lifelong learning society, they have many changes to make. On its present course, the higher education system risks creating a category of learners academically suited to degree study but relegated to other forms of education, less valuable to them economically and less satisfying to them intellectually.

It is possible to integrate adults into degree programs. The University of Toronto has come very close to doing it and should continue to lead the way by building upon 20 years of success in accommodating adult learners.

The U of T has an excellent framework already in place upon which to construct a system which truly integrates the increasingly compatible goals of educating both young people and adults. It has resisted the temptation to treat part-time students as "separate but equal" (a term which was used to describe one method of dealing with part-time students during the debate over integration in the 1970s), instead treating them as distinct but equal. It is a subtle semantic difference that has profound policy implications. To separate part-time students is to restrict their flexibility. The arbitrary definitions of part- and full-time become much more meaningful, creating walls between groups of students that serve only to limit their mobility. Instead, the University of Toronto has tried to meet the truly distinct needs of part-time students but, in all other ways, to grant them the privileges and responsibilities of being a University of Toronto student.

Twenty-five years of persistent organized lobbying by part-time students, and their friends throughout the University, have shown the University of Toronto what its adult learners need to succeed. After a decade of financial pressures felt by every division at the University, perhaps it is a miracle that the programs and services for part-time students remain largely intact. But the U of T status quo will not be able to deal with the challenge of integrating a new influx of adult learners.

When, and if, adult learners return to the University of Toronto, they will be very different than those who came 25 years ago. Many more will expect an economic return on their educational investment, if only to remain competitive. More will be entering the university system for the first time. More will lack even the normal academic prerequisites for direct entry. If these students are disappointed, they will be even more vociferous in their frustration than today's students because dropping-out will be less of an option in the new economy.

The current funding relationship between Ontario universities and the provincial government provides little incentive for universities to renew and enhance their commitment to lifelong learning. Each part-time student is treated as a portion of a funding unit, depending on the course load of the student. For a student taking one course, a university receives one-fifth what it receives for a full-time student. This system makes sense only in so far as the part-time student is assumed to require only one-fifth as much teaching, photocopying, library materials, and so on. But there are many more ways in which the part-time student does not imply the merely partial use of resources. The part-time student may in fact represent a full client at a registrar's office, a full computer record in a database, a full patient at a campus health clinic. Only their impact on the classroom is pro-rated. In most other ways, they represent a complete unit in the university community, placing more than pro-rated demands on university services, administration and infrastructure.

Much of what the University of Toronto has been able to do to enhance opportunities for adult learners was done in spite of government policies which deter such innovation. High enrolment levels in the Summer Session made it possible to pay for the variety of courses offered then. There are no special funding incentives to promote Summer Session growth. Woodsworth College's Pre-University Programme, a highly successful bridging program for applicants lacking the proper high school prerequisites for undergraduate study, is entirely self-funded. The Province, as a matter of explicit policy, provides no resources to this program. Any changes to student services to accommodate part-time students will be financed by the students themselves, either through user fees or campus-wide incidental fees. Child care for faculty and staff, for example, is marginally subsidized by the University, while child care for students is subsidized by the students themselves.

The University needs to reach out and build partnerships

to support its efforts to serve adult and part-time students. The University can provide the innovation in programming, a new philosophy in student and academic services and the mechanisms for facilitating entry into the university system. But it needs business and other employers to provide opportunities for adults to return, to integrate education into the work week and to support their employees' efforts. The University also needs government to provide a practical and well-designed student assistance program and to compensate the University financially in its efforts to broaden the base of adult learners.

Twenty-five years ago, part-time students rebelled against a growing tendency to label them "adult students" engaged in "continuing education". They were simply undergraduate students, they argued, the only thing distinguishing them from full-time students being their reduced course load. This strategy proved largely successful in casting aside any notions of academic inferiority and served its purpose in achieving an integrated system of programs. However, in emphasizing equality, the students had minimized the important differences between themselves and their full-time counterparts, allowing some divisions of the University to define "access" as a simple policy of open doors. Although a 10:00 a.m. Physics lab is "open" to all students, it is largely inaccessible to those who work during the day. In the 1990s, it has become necessary to re-emphasize the distinct needs of adult part-time students.

Through the work of Woodsworth College, and APUS, the

definition of access has broadened to include measures to reduce the barriers to education for adults.

Fortunately, in the near future it may no longer be necessary to emphasize the differences between young people and adults in the context of higher education. Young students are displaying increasing adult-like behaviour in their patterns of work, study and family responsibilities. More and more younger students work, full- and part-time, have children, take evening and summer courses and are pressed for time in between.

Adult students have a new ally in their efforts to create a university environment which can accommodate the contemporary student. For the first time, it may now be possible to create a university environment which works for both full- and part-time students, of any background, of any stage of life. The first step in meeting the needs of a lifelong learning society is for universities, governments and business to listen and respond to the frustrations of the students themselves. I hope this book will move us in that direction.

Bibliography

Anisef, Paul. *Part-time University Students in Canada: An Analysis of the 1974-75 and 1983-84 Postsecondary Student Surveys*. Canadian Organization of Part-time University Students. Ottawa: 1987.

Association of Part-time Undergraduate Students. "APUS Response to the PACE Report". Toronto: December, 1971.

Association of Part-time Undergraduate Students. *The APUS Student Survey*. Toronto: 1991.

Association of Universities and Colleges of Canada. *Trends: The Canadian University in Profile*. Ottawa: 1990.

Association of Universities and Colleges of Canada. "University Planner" in *Saturday Night* September, 1994.

Belanger, R. et al. *Part-time Degree Students: Tommorrow's Majority?* Ottawa: Ministry of Supply and Services Canada (Statistics Canada), 1982.

Blyth, J.A. *A Foundling at Varsity: A History of the Division of University Extension, University of Toronto*. School of Continuing Studies, Toronto: 1976.

Campbell, Duncan D. *The New Majority: Adult Learners in the University*. Edmonton: The University of Alberta Press, 1984.

Erindale College, Undergraduate Studies Committee. "Erindale Response to the PACE Report". Toronto: January, 1972.

Gruetzner, E.M. Report of the Acting Director of the Division of University Extension, in *The President's Report* 1970-71: p. 83-86.

Gruetzner, E.M. Report of the Acting Director of the Division of University Extension, in *The President's Report* 1971-72: p. 79-86.

Innis College Council. Minutes of the Meeting of December 14, 1971.

Levin, Benjamin. "Tuition Fees and University Accessibility" in *Canadian Public Policy*. Vol XVI, No 1, March 1990: p. 51-59.

Ministry of Human Resources Development Canada. *Youth Unemployment and Learning Strategy: Backgrounder*. Ottawa: January, 1994.

Nowlan, David M. *Universities and Economic Renewal*. Toronto: Council of Ontario Universities, 1993.

Ontario Council of University Affairs. *Sustaining Quality in Changing Times: Funding Ontario Universities.* Toronto: August, 1994.

Presidential Advisory Committee on Extension. *Report.* University of Toronto: July, 1970.

Russell, P.H., and the Subcommittee to Advise on the Improvement of the Part-time Degree Programme in Arts and Science. *Report.* University of Toronto: March, 1972.

Statistics Canada. *Education in Canada 1991-92.* Ottawa: 1992.

Statistics Canada. *Universities: Enrolment and Degrees 1991-92.* Ottawa: 1992.

Statistics Canada. *Universities: Enrolment and Degrees 1991-92.* Ottawa: 1994.

Sunter, Deborah. "Youths — Waiting It Out" in *Perspectives.* Statistics Canada: Spring, 1994.

Thompson, Gordon and Larry Devlin. "Access by Part-time Students: A question of openness in Canadian universities." in *The Canadian Journal of Higher Education.* Vol.XXII-3, 1992: p. 57-76.

University of Toronto, Office of the Provost. *Planning for 2000: A Provostial White Paper on University Objectives.* Toronto: February, 1994.

Index